MW00462733

On Womanhood
Connecting and Thriving in Every Season

A Collection of Essays

By

Focused Writers

Foreword by Daphne Maxwell Reid

SPRINGROCK
PUBLISHING

On Womanhood: Connecting and Thriving in Every Season
Copyright © 2022 Focused Writers Membership Community

Founder and Lead Editor: Stacy Hawkins Adams

Writers: Stacy Hawkins Adams, Nailah-Benā Chambers, Margo
Clifford, Jacqueline Hunter, Wanda S. Lloyd, Rita Flores Moore,
Jacqueline J. Owensby, DaNika Neblett Robinson, Njeri Mathis
Rutledge, Belinda Todd, Cassie Edwards Whitlow

Cover Artist: Dawn Edge Campbell

Library of Congress Cataloging-in-Publication Data has been
applied for:
ISBN 978-0-578-36433-9 (hardcover)
ISBN 978-0-578-36434-6 (ebook)

On Womanhood
Connecting and Thriving in Every Season

A Collection of Essays

By

Focused Writers

Stacy Hawkins Adams

Nailah-Benā Chambers**

Jackie Hunter

Rita Flores Moore

DaNika Neblett Robinson

Belinda Todd

Dawn Edge Campbell*

Margo Clifford

Wanda S. Lloyd

Jacqueline J. Owensby

Njeri Mathis Rutledge

Cassie Edwards Whitlow

*Cover artist
** Guest writer

Foreword

Gathering my thoughts on the concept of womanhood aroused a joy in me — a joy that has accumulated since I entered adulthood experiencing life as a grown woman with my mother's love, wisdom, and lessons to anchor me. I was shaped early on by her teachings to recognize my individual blessings and strengths and to use them in the pursuit of finding the purpose for my journey through life.

I've long heeded her words and have shared them many times over with the women I've nurtured, mentored, and befriended. My years of living, loving, modeling, acting, mothering, cooking, sewing, traveling, writing, and more have taught me that only time can reveal the myriad of purposes that one's journey will manifest. When we're willing to live into our womanhood, we'll summon the strength, courage, resilience, and sometimes the sense of adventure required to pursue each leg of the journey with the joy of knowing that we are growing in strength and fortitude.

Contained in this anthology are the experiences of women who have chosen to share how life's glories and challenges—and lessons and blessings—have shaped their journeys into and through womanhood—journeys that are still unfolding.

You may recognize some similarities between their experiences and yours, and perhaps differences in choices, but what these writers and I hope you'll appreciate after reading this book is that great value is inherent in our womanhood. We must continue to trust our individual journeys while encouraging our daughters, sisters, nieces, granddaughters, and female friends to recognize their worth and live life to the fullest, daring to accept the power of their womanhood.

Daphne Maxwell Reid
Actress, Author, Photographer

Contents

Contents

Introduction

Womanhood means different things to different people, but one thing is undeniable and has even been affirmed by archaeologists, sociologists, cultural anthropologists, and the like: Women are the foundation of civilization's steadiness and steadfastness—from the roles they play in bearing and nurturing children to the nurturing and caretaking of their families and friends to the teaching of life lessons and cultural norms for youth and other women in their spheres of influence.

I learned about much of this foundation through my graduate degree studies which earned me a Master of Liberal Arts with an emphasis on women's leadership. What's also true and more relevant, however, is that as a woman myself, I've seen these realities lived many times over, in my personal life as well as in my work as a writer, crafting journalistic stories about women from all walks of life and fiction about women seeking to

1

better understand themselves and others.

Indeed, it is my work as a novelist that most directly led to this intimate book of inspiring essays you're preparing to read. During one of the most fulfilling seasons of my life as an author, when I was writing multiple books while also working part- or full-time, raising a young family, and volunteering in my community, I was receiving numerous queries from aspiring authors about how to get started and go the distance with their writing projects. I often taught at writing conferences locally and around the nation, yet these individual requests were pouring in at a rate that I didn't have the bandwidth to manage.

My initial solution was to launch a six-week teleseminar program for aspiring fiction and nonfiction writers that I could teach from the comfort of my home, and they could participate from anywhere in the world. That effort, Author In You, flourished for several years. Still, I found myself answering more and more "one-off" questions that didn't necessarily require a lengthy course or a formal writing or marketing consultation, so I decided to launch an online membership community through which participants could pay a small fee to have ready access to me for questions, while also learning from and growing with like-minded individuals. The Focused Writers Membership Community officially took off in July 2015. Fast forward to today (2022), and I'm grateful to share that the Focused Writers community is thriving.

This grassroots mentorship group includes a mighty band of about a dozen members (give or take), who regularly connect with me and with each other on social media, meet once a month on a live call or in a virtual meeting space, and occasionally gather in person. Group members just happen to be all female at this juncture, and they span in age from their late twenties to their early seventies. Members live in Virginia (where I'm based), Texas, Georgia, North Carolina, and Nevada.

Our tribe not only focuses on writing, but also

has become a support group of sorts for whatever our members are going through while attempting to write. This led to conversations among members a few years ago about producing something special together. Someone floated the idea of a podcast and another kept mentioning an anthology, and finally, the group decided to move forward with the book idea—or rather, they convinced me to move forward.

I agreed, as long as we would walk through each step of the process together, from selecting a theme to writing individual essays to helping with editing, weighing in on the cover design, choosing publication platforms and learning how to promote and raise awareness about the book. All of these endeavors would be teachable (and bonding) moments on the journey to publication.

They said yes, and here we are, with you now holding, or reading on a digital device, the compilation of essays that our group, the Focused Writers, poured our hearts and teamwork into producing.

We chose the theme and title *On Womanhood* because what we've learned in our years together of writing, procrastinating on writing, dealing with life while writing, putting writing on hold to deal with life, and everything in between is that our standing together and supporting one another has been just as important as having a creative process in and of itself. We wanted to write a book about our individual experiences as women on the journey to living life fully and as fabulously as possible, and one that would encourage you and other readers to unfold yourselves and do the same.

In addition to most of the current Focused Writers being featured in this collection of personal and heartfelt essays, we have a guest writer, a college student who is on her way to becoming and already thriving in the process. And our cover was designed by a Focused Writer member who also is a talented artist, telling stories through her visual creations.

We hope you'll enjoy this book, which reflects

the radiance and variance of who we are as women, and as (mostly, but not all) women of color. These essays signal and celebrate our uniqueness, and we hope you'll also find some important universal truths illuminated throughout, to reinforce that whoever you are and whatever season of life you're experiencing, there is always hope and an inner flame to guide you toward your possibilities, your purpose, and your power. *On Womanhood* is our collective love offering toward that goal. Enjoy and be blessed!

Stacy Hawkins Adams
Focused Writers Founder,
Author, and Writing Mentor

*"Experiencing womanhood
to the fullest means
building something every day
with our thoughts and choices."*

Choose Today What You'll Live with Tomorrow

By Rita Flores Moore

As women, we are life givers and nurturers. Every day we are given opportunities to choose what we know is good and right for ourselves, and eventually for many of us, our families. Life is complicated enough without getting caught up in cycles of uncertainty and regret. With this in mind, it's important that as often as possible, we consider our gifts, our talents, and our purpose when deciding to which things we'll say yes, no, or maybe. There must be a purpose in what we do or say because so much hangs in the balance of the decisions we make.

Some of us live life carefree, without much thought to the consequences, with a belief that what will be will be; while others of us are so afraid that we rarely venture outside of our known and normal—the places that make us feel safest or most in control. But what if we considered a happy medium is to fully consider all of our options—our choices—and weigh the pros and cons in ways that help us to be responsible, yet also live fully? As a professional speaker and writer, my passion is to help guide women to make better decisions, to choose more wisely.

Experiencing womanhood to the fullest means building something every day with our thoughts and choices. We choose who and what we allow into our hearts and minds, who has voice in our decisions, what we laugh at, and how we spend our time. The more important the decision, the more we may struggle over whether we're making the right one.

This is not unusual, according to some of the leading voices on womanhood, including Sheryl Sandberg, chief operating officer of Facebook and author of the bestselling book about women leaders, *Lean In*; Brené Brown, bestselling author of numerous books about vulnerability and choices, and Valorie Burton, a bestselling author and life coach who speaks often about life balance and goal setting for women.

The fact that these women writers have forged careers on helping women own their power and make wiser choices is proof that it's an issue many more of us should address with confidence and courage. In my case, I've become passionate about this because, as a woman in her early seventies, I often reflect on decisions I made decades earlier that continue to impact who I am and how I show up in the world today. Do I have regrets? Sure—no one gets through life without a few. Yet, I also have choices for which I'm very grateful, including those that have given me beautiful children and grandchildren, a chance to live my dream of public speaking, and opportunities to travel the world.

In many ways, I'm no different than you—except in the ways that matter. You are uniquely designed to live a life and fulfill a purpose that only you can achieve, and this journey starts with the questions you ask yourself and the choices you make as a result.

Think about what questions you can ask yourself that will lead to choices to improve your life and the lives of those around you. And guess what? Good questions lead to good decisions. Your questions should reflect your character and your integrity.

For example, if you are a law-abiding citizen, you won't make choices that break the law, even if they result in abundant income. If you believe in loyalty and commitment, you'll choose to stay true to a friend rather than benefit from a choice that could greatly reward you while causing that person harm. Keep in mind that even your responses to someone else's decisions are choices that will become part of the story your character tells. It's a good idea to always ask yourself what stories you want to tell with your choices.

I recall a choice I made early in my marriage. My husband and I spent a lot of time with other young married couples. No matter where we went, women and men would always end up gathering in separate rooms. The women would talk about their husbands and the silly things their men would do. Rarely did I hear someone say something positive.

One consistent complaint was that men leave the toilet seat up, although that sort of thing never bothered me. I don't walk into a bathroom backwards, and if I walk in and see the toilet seat up, I drop it and use it—no big deal.

The stories shared by some of the women in our group were always silly to me, so I rarely had anything to say. Soon, I began to feel left out. One evening the ladies were discussing something my husband and I had recently dealt with, and I decided to share part of our story.

The next day, my husband asked me if I had shared the story with the ladies. I said yes, I shared part of what happened. One of his friends had obviously repeated it to him, and I could see that my husband was embarrassed and hurt. I made the wrong choice, and I lost his trust. I had betrayed him.

That's when I learned a valuable lesson: never break trust. Part of working on a relationship—any relationship (marriage, family, friendship, business)—is trust. There is safety in being in a relationship, and it is only as strong as the trust of both parties. Knowing that you can be trusted is a valuable attribute.

Ask yourself, what is your motive when deciding what you will share with others. Don't choose to fit in by telling stories and betraying trust. Sometimes it's best to be a story keeper, not a storyteller. Protect trust and protect your character, one decision at a time. We might not know what hangs in the balance of a decision we make, but we do know that private decisions have public outcomes.

Consider, for example, a decision to divorce your spouse. Your private decisions more than likely won't stay private, and personal decisions will impact others, especially if children are involved.

Choice is a huge power. The power of the choices you make leads to infinite circumstances that can affect your legacy. Things like, "Should I go to school today?" or "Should I eat junk food for lunch?" are actually small choices that might not seem to matter so much. But think about it: Even those small habits lead you down a path that could change your more important and lasting choices.

Missing school here or there on the wrong day could cost you a test grade or a chance visit with a college rep for your desired school. Eating junk food for lunch on a regular basis could impact your health. These are seemingly simple choices in isolation—which they are, if they occur every so often. But when choices become habits, one should make sure they are the choices and habits you want to stand by.

The most important choices will require asking yourself, *Will my decision pass on wisdom or will it pass on suffering?*

I am reminded of a story about a woman who would always cut her ham in half before cooking it. Her husband asked her why she always cut the ham in half. She told him that's how her mother always prepared it so that's how she did it.

Later, when the woman had the opportunity, she asked her mother, "Why do we always cut the ham in half before cooking it?" Her mother said "I always cut it in half because I never had a pan large enough to cook it whole." That's a simple example of doing things the way we do them because that's how it has always been done.

Because I believe that better decisions lead to fewer regrets, I often share five key questions to ask when you have a decision to make.

The first question has to do with **integrity.** Ask, *Am I being truly honest with myself?* Dishonest people suffer because their mind and body know they are lying. Live a life of integrity. Liars don't heal. Excellence in character, conduct, and commitment will lead to a happy life. Know yourself, who you are, and what you want. If it triggers fear or shame, don't do it.

If you are not sure of what you want or if you need help to determine your next move, ask yourself: *Will this make me happy? Will I enjoy this? Will this hurt me or anyone else?* If it's something you don't want anyone to ever know, ask yourself: *Will anyone find out?* Remember, you are focused on the story your life will tell about your womanhood. Protect your integrity.

The second question has to do with **leaving a legacy.** What story do you want to tell? Most people say they want to leave some sort of legacy in life. We all want to be remembered, because being remembered means that our lives have had meaning and significance to others. One bad decision can destroy everything you've worked for, and one single choice you make today can change your legacy. Ask yourself these questions: *How do I want to be remembered? Will generations follow me and know that I've been here? What have I done that has never been done before?* You might never know who may benefit from the legacy you leave.

The third question is about your **conscience**. Ask yourself: *Is this something that deserves my attention?* Your response should be in line with your values. If your decision has a public outcome, ask yourself: *What is a wise thing to do? In light of my past experiences and my circumstances, what's best for me?* Also, do a self-audit. What's working for you and what isn't? If you feel resistant, why is that? Are you holding yourself hostage? Clear your conscience by asking what feels right. Follow that feeling; it's your freedom.

The fourth question has to do with **maturity**. What is the wise thing to do? For example, one universal experience most of us have had is knowing someone who does not keep their commitments. This shows a lack of maturity. Honor your commitments. Always stick with your word. If you tell someone you're going to do something, do it, or run the risk of breaking his or her heart by letting that person down.

The fifth and final question is about how you will acquire and maintain a loving **relationship** with a partner or spouse. Ask yourself: *What does love require of me?* Consider the consequences of your goals or your dreams if you were to make the wrong choice. Keep working on yourself. Fall madly in love with yourself first, then you will be ready for someone else to love you. Love yourself so much that you're willing to wait for what you deserve. Love yourself enough not to settle. If you act desperate, you look desperate. That's not a good choice.

You are who you are today because of all the choices you've made in your life. Make one good decision after another. One right choice, then the next right choice, then the next. Strive for excellence in character, conduct, integrity, and commitment. Embrace your womanhood.

In one of her books, author J.K. Rowling described: "It is our choices, Harry, that show what we truly are, far more than our abilities."

You will know you did the right thing when, in the end, there is peace. We can live in peace and wisdom, or we can live in bondage and captivity. There is wisdom in waiting. Wise women listen to each other's counsel. That is a sign of true womanhood.

Journaling Break

*"My ability to be present
for my sister was key.
She deserved to be
embraced in love."*

Journey with My Sister
By Margo Clifford

Everything changed with a phone call. On the other end of the line was my sister, Mary. "It's breast cancer," she said softly, weeping through her words.

I choked out words of support between my own sobs. What we had all feared but didn't want to think about had come true. Her biopsy came back positive for HER2 negative, estrogen positive breast cancer.

"Whatever you need," I promised at the end of the phone call. "Whatever you want. I'll be there for you." Thus began my sister's fourteen-year journey battling breast cancer.

According to the Breast Cancer Coalition, one in eight women is diagnosed with breast cancer each year in the United States. The odds are you will know someone diagnosed and may help them face the challenges battling this disease.

I became a member of my youngest sister's support team in the fall of 2006. The week before Mary's diagnosis, I had accompanied her to the hospital for a lump to be removed. I didn't realize it at the time, but this would be the beginning of many visits to hospitals, clinics, and doctors' offices. The complex path of dealing with cancer was filled with peaks, valleys, and wait stops.

Her chemo treatments, poor test results, and the cancer's recurrence became the valleys along the way.

The peaks were those scans declaring the cancer was in remission or the new chemo drug stalling the spread. The wait stops were the long stretches in between the peaks and valleys. Wait to be tested and then wait sometimes days or weeks for lab results. Wait for treatments to end so she would feel better. Wait to feel better so she could resume family activities. Mary traveled through a long mountain range of peaks, valleys, and wait stops.

The cumulative side effects of chemo made it difficult for my sister to care for her daughters, who were then one and six years old. My beloved brother-in-law, Worth, could cover all the bases on weekends, but during the week, he commuted for work an hour each way from their home outside of Baltimore to Washington, DC.

Mary's immediate family needed support to ease the burden of the everyday. The grandparents came to the rescue. My folks and my brother-in-law's parents took turns staying a month at a time. The multiple benefits with the new living arrangement presented surprise gifts along the way.

Mary's girls developed a closer relationship with their grandparents, none of whom lived nearby. The family had the help they needed to get through each day, and grandparents were part of the day-to-day occurrences in my nieces' lives. Without this unfortunate event, which brought them together under one roof, the girls' time with their grandparents might never have happened.

Making meals, doing laundry, waiting for the school bus, taking the girls to their appointments, and play dates were maintained. My sister's goal was to keep the girls' lives as normal as possible, so our families took up the charge to do whatever we could.

During the times of waiting, both sides of the family became masters of distraction for Mary. We would scour the internet for ideas to help keep her mind off what might be looming ahead. *What needs to be done in the house? What can we bake? Let's go shopping. Have you seen this new series on cable? Check out this new home decorating catalog.*

Inspired by Pinterest, Mary enlisted us to be her "Home Enhancement Assistants." We organized, painted, and fixed up the laundry room and the girls' craft room in the basement. Worth's mom added her creative touches to the kitchen and dining room. Cathy, my other sister; my mom; and I helped decorate for the holidays. We put up lights, made wreaths, and saw that every corner of the house was filled with holiday cheer.

We binge-watched Hallmark Channel Christmas shows. I made Hallmark movie bingo cards and distributed them among the family. Hallmark holiday movies have many elements in common. *Did the movie include a gingerbread house contest, secret cookie recipe, ice skating, a cute dog, or high school sweethearts reconnecting?* I would get text messages from Mary when she got bingo. Whatever would bring a smile to my sister's face was all I wanted to do.

Mary had about eight good years of traveling through the peaks of her journey. The times when the cancer was in remission allowed for many family trips to visit grandparents, cousins, aunts, and uncles. Making memories was the primary goal along with endless Monopoly games, arts and crafts projects, cooking with the grandmothers, and having "Camp Clifford" at my brother Tom's house. The girls learned paddle boarding and kayaking, played tennis, and went biking. It was a time for life to become more normal again without weekly infusions, daily nausea, or extreme exhaustion.

What became important was celebrating in the now. During holidays, our families had a heightened sense of being present in the moment. No longer would I go through the motions of the holiday, but I focused on being present. During those celebrations, we spent a lot of time reminiscing about our childhood. Tom, Cathy, and I loved talking about how our timid, shy Mary got the lead in the high school musical *Oliver*, even though none of us had ever heard her sing before. We recalled how awestruck we were when Mary took the stage and confidently belted out her first song. The gutsy kid on stage was a side of her we had never seen.

Mary's hidden courage would be called forth many times along the journey with cancer. We realized that being together as a family gave us the strength we needed. The gatherings gave us a you-can-do-this shot in the arm. Mary loved it.

Even through the good times, nothing ever really took away the dark cloud casting a shadow over Mary's path. It contained all the worries and fears surrounding her illness. There were times when fears could be ignored, but they were always there, hovering.

My sister was concerned most about her daughters and her husband. She worried about the toll her health would take on her family and the possibility that the medical interventions would not be enough to stop the cancer from spreading.

The valley parts of the journey were the hardest. It was difficult watching my baby sister deal with the adverse effects of treatments and the letdown when drug trials didn't work. I felt helpless in the valleys.

As the big sister, I was supposed to fix things, make it all better. Growing up, I always had the answers. When Mary needed help on a school project, boyfriend advice, or support dealing with friends, I was there for her. However, this time, not only did I not have all the answers, I didn't have the cure. I didn't know how to help her.

She showed me what she needed most. When the cancer came back, she wanted me to just be there, to sit with her. Knowing she was not facing this alone was a great comfort to Mary. While waiting for her infusions, I scoped out a quiet place in the medical center where we could just sit, undisturbed. We talked if she wanted to talk; when she didn't, we sat in silence.

Sometimes, we would read or nap. The perfect spot happened to be on the tenth floor of the cancer center that overlooked Baltimore's Inner Harbor. The day consisted of appointments and then the infusion, about nine hours total. Between appointments, we watched the ships come and go from the harbor, the bustle of cars and people on the street below, and then the best part when the sun turned the buildings gold at sunset. Even in a center dealing with terminal illness, we found a gift.

The American Society of Clinical Oncology points out that to support someone going through cancer treatment, there are several things to consider. It's important to process your own feelings as a supporter, learn about the diagnosis and think about things from a friend or family member's perspective. Fortunately, I was able to depend on close friends who gave me opportunities to process my feelings.

Mary's journey was about *her* needs, not about mine. She didn't need to listen to my worries, my sadness, my fears about her diagnosis and treatment. Through many walk-and-talks, I came to grips with the finality of her terminal illness. My ability to be present for my sister was key. She deserved to be embraced in love.

Mary's desire was to stay at home surrounded by family as long as she could. Her goal was to fight until the end, and that's exactly what she did. We kept her company and told her how much we loved her. And when the time came, Mary passed away in her own bed, not the hospital bed that had just been set up in the den a few hours earlier. She never wanted to leave her family, succumb to this disease, or give up on life.

My little sister became a warrior on the day of her diagnosis. She bravely marched through difficult and seemingly impossible terrain. I know now that Mary's strength through this stormy journey helped me when I thought I was supposed to be strong for her. She was the guide throughout all of it. I miss her terribly, but I see her strength and determination in her daughters. And I carry it with me forever.

*"In my desperation,
I listened, and that's when
my life began turning around."*

Taking Care of All of Me

By Cassie Edwards Whitlow

I don't do therapy. I have Jesus.

How many times have we heard or even spoken those words?

I am a huge fan of Jesus. I've been in church my whole life, I've had a great life, and I believe Jesus can fix it for you, as the old hymn goes.

However, becoming a mother of two about a decade ago made me enter into a season of life that prayer and I couldn't handle alone. That realization struck me when my firstborn, my son Nathan, turned three. I could tell by his timid interactions with other kids his age and by what appeared to be developmental delays that there was something "different" about him.

By the time he was four, my personal detective work had me suspecting he had autism, a developmental disorder that usually begins in early childhood and is characterized by impaired communication and emotional detachment. Years of testing began, and along with questions from preschool teachers and others about his "behavior problems," and when he was seven, we received official confirmation that he was indeed autistic.

My world fell apart.

Along with the fear and grief that this new territory brought came looming doubts about my ability to not only meet my son's needs, but also to make sure that he felt loved—and happy.

I gave him love and discipline. I read to him, talked to him, taught him about Jesus. I consumed books about parenting to educate myself, but still, my inadequacy lingered, and it seemed like Nathan could feel it.

The worst part was the looks I got from adults whenever Nathan would have a meltdown in public. You know, from the parents who had raised their "perfect" children perfectly.

Some of them would say things like, "There's nothing wrong with him. He just needs a good whooping" or "Give me about ten minutes with him, and he won't have any more tantrums."

I eventually learned to ignore the noise, but for a young mother who already felt lost and alone as a military wife living far away from home and family, I felt like I was failing — as a parent (and also in life). I didn't ask for much help because even though I craved it, I was embarrassed that I couldn't do this alone when my husband was deployed, or even when he was home. I should be able to handle this, I thought. After all, there were people dealing with way more important challenges.

As much as I beat myself up, however, hindsight has helped me see that in doing all I knew to do at that time, I was doing right by Nathan. In the year after his diagnosis, we had moved from Virginia to London, England, and when I realized that Nathan would receive more appropriate developmental and academic support stateside, my husband willingly asked for a transfer.

We landed in Las Vegas, where we currently live, and while the move turned out to be an excellent fit for Nathan's growth and progress, it also has been excellent for mine. For it was here that I realized that I need help, too.

Things were actually going really well when the breakthrough occurred. I found a job that I enjoyed, and my children were thriving in school. Even more miraculously, I had just survived a brain tumor that could have killed me.

I should have been feeling on top of the world, yet no matter how hard I tried to force myself to feel great, feelings of defeat consumed me. One day as I was driving home from work, I realized I should have gotten off the highway three exits back. I turned around as soon as I could, but I missed my exit again. This had been happening often, and I also was making careless mistakes at work.

When I got home that evening, all I could do was lie in bed. I began turning down social invitations and feeding my family fast food more often. When my husband came home from work one evening and found me curled up on the floor crying, he convinced me to see a therapist.

In my desperation, I listened, and that's when my life began turning around. It wasn't easy, though.

While therapy was one of the best decisions I could have made for myself, there were times when I couldn't handle all of the "stuff" therapy was bringing up. Sometimes I wouldn't go, and at one point, I stopped going altogether.

Several months later, I found the courage to pick up where I left off, dealing with childhood traumas and even some adult-experienced rejection as a military wife and mom. This time I kept going, and within in a year, I was on the road to finding myself and to discovering my purpose.

Dealing with childhood trauma is not easy. I'm not quite there yet. I've lived with trauma all these years. Now I have been given a second chance at healing. From now on, my mental health will get the same attention as my physical health and my spiritual health.

After a few years of mental health care, Nathan is also doing quite well in all areas of his life. A happy child makes for an even happier mom.

What have I learned from all of this? That life is a journey, and while I'll always have King Jesus with me, it's also okay to find other meaningful ways to care for, nurture, and heal myself. God doesn't have to be left out of the equation; in fact, He often puts healers in our path.

Journaling Break

*"Silence was the way
my family communicated,
as if we didn't talk about a problem,
it did not exist."*

When Silence Is Not Golden
By Belinda Todd

It happened when I was least expecting it. I was passing through the foyer glancing sideways at the mirror when I saw my mother—in me. When did I become my mother? Had I always looked this much like her?

Swiss psychologist Carl Jung contended that what you resist persists. Unresolved emotional issues that are not faced will not only plague you, they will grow like unwanted weeds, invading the garden of your mind.

I had a complicated relationship with my mother for most of my life. I loved her—her laughter at telling a funny joke, for example, and her little ways of bringing sunshine into our lives, such as baking a cake just because it was your favorite. I also adored her spunk, always taking life head-on. When there were situations that could have demoralized her, she showed her ability to bounce back without penalty.

Raising four girls could not have been easy. My mother was common-sense smart and used her savvy to hold down good jobs for low wages. Layoffs would leave our family finances frazzled, but somehow, we always made it. My father worked steadily for many years in the same government job, but when my parents divorced, it placed even more pressure on her to make ends meet. With the help of child support and loving grandparents, we made it, even though I remember that we lived a month-to-month existence.

I always knew my mother loved us, but as I became older, I did not feel evidence of that love. It would be years before I could intelligently examine those feelings and recognize that what I was craving was emotional closeness. I eventually understood that what I was seeking was a low priority for my mother, while working long hours to keep food on the table and a roof over our heads.

Feelings of insecurity and low self-confidence were ignited around age ten when I overheard in an adult conversation that I was "illegitimate." The man I knew as my father was not my biological father, they said. Later that night, I looked up that word. *Illegitimate: Born out of wedlock. Born to parents not married to each other. Unlawful. Illegal.*

That word changed my world.

There was no way to unhear the message. No take backs. The word imprinted itself in my young mind, and the corresponding vibrations of that message spread through my entire being. I translated it to mean I was unloved by my biological father, who must not have wanted me. I was not good enough. I was not really wanted, and I would have to work hard to earn my rightful place in the family. My three sisters were much younger than me, and the father we'd all known was indeed their dad, so this crushing revelation was mine to bear alone.

Not only were those messages of shame the loudest voices in my head, I also felt my mother was to blame for my situation. Gradually and subconsciously, the tension between us flared. My rebellion began, and the itch to feel loved and desirable continued to grow.

The story is common. As a teen, I began to look for love in all the wrong places. At the same time, I was an honor student and I earned a full scholarship to attend college away from home. Yet, I was a mess.

Years later, as I was leading a full life as a flight attendant for a major airline, I seldom returned home to visit. I always sent gifts to my much younger sisters and helped them financially, but in some ways, I began to practice the same emotional distance with them that I'd felt from our mother.

My mother would occasionally visit me in Atlanta, and I took her on wonderful vacations to Las Vegas, Hawaii, and England that earned *oohs* and *aahs* from her girlfriends. But she and I never had serious discussions about the elephant in the room. We never talked about my biological father.

Silence was the way my family communicated, as if we didn't talk about a problem, it did not exist. My mother never broached the subject of who my father was. Nor did I. I wanted to know who he was in her life and whether he ever acknowledged my existence. I wanted to know if he loved me.

Years later, when I finally summoned the courage to bring it up, my mother deflected my questions. She acted as if she couldn't understand why I was just now asking her about this rather than responding with details or offering context.

Don Miguel, author of *The Four Agreements,* wrote, "Ninety-five percent of the beliefs we have stored in our minds are nothing but lies, and we suffer because we believe all these lies." Because of the lack of answers, I suffered in my mind because I believed the lie that I wasn't valuable.

A few years after that unsuccessful attempt to secure answers from my mother, when I was about thirty years old, I married the proverbial tall, dark, and handsome man who I thought would give me the love and validation I craved. If I knew then what I know now, I would have added much more to my wish list for a mate. My husband was kind and caring, but he had his own set of unresolved issues.

One thing we did well was create a beautiful, healthy son. However, becoming a mother left me with questions about my lineage, and I wondered about the genetic traits in my father and his family. For the first time, I felt an urgency to know more about him.

When my son was six years old, he and I moved back to my Virginia hometown, a move that years earlier I would have sworn would not happen.

I wish I could say that my mother and I had resolved our issues by then, but the truth is, I was difficult to love and not easy to please. I was still holding that subconscious grudge because of that word that had burdened me so long ago.

When I asked my mother again about my biological father, this time she shared a few details, and eventually she suggested that I speak to my father's sister, a woman named Helen who was also one of her card-playing friends.

That visit with Helen did not go well. While she may not have intended to be, she was unkind. Her remarks were harsh and bruising, and she didn't provide me with any of the answers I sought. The conversation ended with her asking me why I wanted someone in my life who had been unavailable to me. I had no reply, and the tears flowed when I returned to my car.

Soon after that, I realized I had to accept my parents' decisions, and I began the work to heal myself. I went to therapy. I returned to the church. I began to feel the love of God in a way I never had before.

Every time I sang the hymns I grew up with, I would weep. Reading the Bible became an experience where verses and messages touched my heart. I had read those verses before, but they never spoke to me like this.

I realized that God was speaking to my heart, cleansing it, and preparing it. The doubt, insecurity, and self-hatred could only be cleansed by the goodness and perfection of my higher power, so I had to make room for God's perfect plan and His timing.

My mother passed away in 2002. Much was still left

unsaid, but I do know she loved me. She met and approved of the man I married months before her passing, my second marriage. Her greatest joys were my son, her first grandchild, and her other two grandchildren. She was very pleased that all four of her girls had gone to college, had successful careers, and made a place for themselves in this world. She would have absolutely loved her namesake Charlotte Ruby, my granddaughter and her great-granddaughter.

I love the words engraved on my mother's headstone: *Her song has ended, but her melody lingers on in our hearts forever.*

Through a series of what I believe are God-ordained events, I eventually met my half-brother, my father's son. We were introduced by a family member who knew about the family relationship.

My half-brother and his wife live in Connecticut. We are developing a relationship and becoming friends.

During one of our first visits, he handed me a large envelope containing a photograph of our now-deceased father. After viewing the picture, I became emotional, and I quickly returned it to the envelope. Never before had I questioned the dimple in my chin. In his own way, part of the father that I never knew was lingering with me, too, just as my mother always would.

Journaling Break

*"Forgiveness is a process
that requires us to work
from the inside out."*

The Power of Forgiveness

By Jacqueline J. Owensby

"To forgive is to set a prisoner free and discover that the prisoner was you." — Lewis B. Smedes

I've always been a daddy's girl. My dad was my hero, my true knight in shining armor. Our close father-daughter relationship brought an element of magic into my life. But my father and I lost that magic when my parents separated.

On a warm summer day when I was about twelve years old, my mother began hauling items to her car. I was told to pack whatever I wanted to bring, no questions entertained, and no justification given.

Completely stripped of all that was familiar, I became guarded and stopped sharing my true feelings. I built a wall around my heart, determined to protect myself from the risks that come with loving someone. I decided to carve my dad out of my life. In my mind, it was his fault that my mother had to leave.

As my high school graduation drew closer, I realized parents don't have all of the answers. I wanted to share my feelings with my dad and tell him I forgave him for not being around during that difficult transition, but by then, my heart was so hardened that I'd stopped crying. I convinced myself I didn't care or need anyone for that matter. My mind was made up, and I was well on my way to making a better life for myself.

As I grew older, it was evident those childhood scars had only deepened and stretched. I was angry, frustrated, and hurt because of the decisions my parents made. However, tragedy has a way of turning things around. Years later, after my parents divorced, Dad had a major heart attack. Still angry and hurt, I wanted to run in the opposite direction, but every time I tried, I felt sadness streaming down the walls of my heart, and soon, tears gliding over my cheeks. I was finally ready to surrender.

I had been caring from afar for the man I refused to forgive for more than half my life. Almost losing him helped me realize that it was okay to love my dad even though he missed out on so much. It became okay to allow him access into my world again because even after everything that happened, all that really matters is love.

After more than forty years, I can say without wavering that I now fully understand how parents do not know everything and how they can make some heart-wrenching mistakes. I can attest to this because, you see, now I am a parent. How absolutely painful it would be for me to have my own children carve me out of their lives because I made some ignorant choices during their youth.

I've also learned over the years that forgiveness is more for the offended than it is for the offender. This simple act brings freedom to live beyond the pain. I can attest that it did for me.

If this is the gospel truth, then why do we struggle with forgiveness? The facts are you were betrayed, taken total advantage of, lied to, talked about, mistreated emotionally, mentally, and perhaps even physically. Well, the truth is also that nothing about considering forgiveness can change this fact. And nothing about considering forgiveness requires us to disregard the hurt, loss, or feelings of abandonment that may be very present. In fact, acknowledging these real experiences of a situation can be necessary steps in the process of healing and releasing.

Of course, we can choose to repeatedly analyze or replay the offense in our minds. Deep down, it may feel good to be fixated on what happened because it feeds that starving rage within. And after all, why should the offended person have to relent? It was the offenders who did the wrong deed. They owe you.

I've heard it said through many church sermons that when we choose to remain offended, feeding off the hurt, we are building a fence. Did you catch that? Offense builds a fence—like the one I had guarding my heart when I remained distant from and furious with my dad for so many years. Yet, could it be that we often hold on to the grudge because we need to have some sort of control?

I know for certain I'm not the only one who has basked in the moment of having leverage over my offender. Truth is, my actions weren't hurting the offender as much as they were harming me.

Unforgiveness works much like fear by paralyzing your entire being, hindering your quality of life, and causing you to become stagnant and unproductive. But if I forgave and released the person, I told myself, then I would no longer have anything to hold on to. It was almost as if my very identity was taking shape around me being the victim. Unforgiveness can also feel like the sandbags attached to a bouquet of helium-filled party balloons. The sandbags are there to keep the balloons grounded. Once they are loosened, the sky is the limit for those balloons. Have you ever noticed how beautifully they rise? The helium gives the balloons lift, just like the hot air being pushed into a hot air balloon. Imagine that unforgiveness is like sandbags and forgiveness is like helium, a source that can help us rise above our circumstances and release our victim status.

If you are still holding on to unforgiveness, this is a good day to decide to release it. You must know that while you will not be able to change others, you have full control over the choices you make. To continue allowing this cankerous wound to thrive within you brings a myriad of emotional, mental, and physical illnesses, such as anxiety, depression, and high blood pressure all of which can ultimately kill you. We must choose to forgive if we want to be free and live beyond the walls and fences we've built.

Forgiveness is a process that requires us to work from the inside out. When we think about the way we learn and grow from unfavorable experiences, it is an inward change that occurs first, then the transformation becomes evident in our outer response. Forgiveness takes all of the offense and resulting torture and morphs it into healing and wholeness.

"The Lord our God is merciful and forgiving, even though we have rebelled against him." —Daniel 9:9

In 2020, my father died due to complications from COVID-19. I'd seen him two months prior to him getting sick, and he was laughing and reminding me to bring him fried chicken on my next visit to the nursing facility where he lived. When it was nearing the end of our visit, Dad insisted the nurse open the door so he could give me a hug and a kiss, despite mandatory social distancing guidelines. Irritated that we couldn't do so, I was pleased to see how calm and settled in his mind he looked. He told me he loved me, and I told him I loved him right back.

When I returned to my car with tears in my eyes because I didn't know when I would be able to hug him or rub his rough hands again, I whispered in my heart once more, "I forgive you Dad, and I love you." Two months later, Dad transitioned from this life to the next. We never got that hug.

The power of forgiveness brings peace, and with that peace, release—release for the one who has held herself captive far too long. It took some time, a process that was very necessary, but I was released from the towering wall that once fenced in my heart because of an offense.

Nelson Mandela, a man fondly remembered as being loving and forgiving, once said, "Forgiveness liberates the soul. It removes fear. That is why it is such a powerful weapon."

When will you decide to pick up your weapon of power—forgiveness? It is time for your soul to be liberated. The power of forgiveness allows you to live a fearless life, without the sandbags.

No longer bound.

Journaling Break

"I'm not sure where this journey of exploration and advocacy is leading. I just know I must keep going because it matters, and so do I."

See Me, Hear Me

By Nailah-Benā Chambers

For all of my K–12 school experience, I was one of a few Black students in my classes. I often felt different, and othered, and it was difficult.

Even so, I excelled academically. Yet, at the same time, some teachers and classmates couldn't handle my boldness. My teachers even told my parents that I was "too much and too aggressive for my classmates." For me, it was confusing and frustrating, constantly having to censor myself and overanalyze everything I said and did at such a young age.

At some point, I gave up on fitting in. I realized that no amount of censorship would allow me to escape my Blackness in such a White environment. Unfortunately, this led me to hold the assumption that my history and my identity were unimportant, both to my teachers and my fellow students. While my assumption was supported multiple times throughout my middle school and high school experiences, it did not stop me from searching for that representation.

Through extracurricular activities, such as participating in an African American social organization for mothers and children called Jack & Jill of America, Inc., and attending a weekly Chinese School to learn Mandarin, for example, I learned to appreciate my culture and the cultures of others and to explore other interests. What this newfound knowledge about myself and my interests brought me was not only a surge in my desire to advocate for myself and other marginalized communities, but also a confidence in myself.

In high school, I created a club centered around inclusion and advocacy for students of color called Diverse Hands at Work. While the club experienced major pushback, it was a huge milestone (and source of support) for me and for the students involved. Additionally, it pushed me to take full advantage of my agency in deciding where I wanted to go to college. I wanted to attend a university that would allow me to focus on my academics and also meet people from around the world and from all walks of life.

I was fortunate enough to have grades that allowed me to have multiple choices. However, I still felt unsure of what was most important when deciding where to go. I was constantly stuck between choosing a university based on demographics or outstanding education. Which was most essential to my academic success and professional development? After deep and lengthy reflection, I decided that my academic success in high school was hindered by the burden of racism and underrepresentation, and that one thing I wanted to worry about less in college was my Blackness, in comparison to others' race.

So when I ended up choosing a diverse university—a predominantly White institution (PWI)—I was excited to finally be represented and meet other Black students who could truly understand the academic journey I've experienced and to meet students of different cultural backgrounds as well. While it was a difficult decision choosing between a predominantly Black university and a PWI, I knew that I needed to branch out of my comfort zone and that being exposed to people with whom I am not familiar would ultimately be most beneficial for me. Being exposed to multiple cultures and identities would expand my view of the world and would allow me to be more in touch with those around me.

When I arrived at the University of Maryland, Baltimore County, in fall 2019, I was eager to apply my knowledge and advocacy skills in the classroom. However, what I found was that while the students were diverse, the professors were overwhelmingly White; and while some were non-binary, transgender, or even neurodivergent, they were still individuals who had not incorporated diverse perspectives into their curricula.

This became an obstacle for me. When I would press for more representation and in-depth discussions of Black history, feminist theories, and perspectives in my classes and in my papers, I was shut down and labeled as a difficult student. In fact, I received reduced credit for the homework assignments I submitted because I chose to discuss the lack of representation and my disappointment with the assignments. In an attempt to broaden the discussion, I was penalized for "not following instructions." I saw my classmates from other cultures experience similar challenges.

One example of this was my Theories of Feminism course, in which we focused on current intersectional approaches and theories of feminism and their impact on movements. On paper, this course was intriguing, and I hoped the outcome would be new perspectives and ideologies that I didn't have before. However, I quickly found that the course was taught from a singular perspective. It seemed sometimes like the professor saw herself in every text we analyzed, and any criticism toward that text was a direct criticism of her and White women as a whole.

I often critiqued the ideologies and opinions of the feminist texts we explored, sharing how I viewed the perspectives of the mostly White scholars and authors as short-sighted. I expressed that some works were harmful to the black and brown students present in class, either because of lack of representation in the assumptions made by the writers or due to subtle or overt stereotypes used in their examples. I expressed how this was not beneficial or helpful for a course that had a focus on intersectionality. Whenever I raised these concerns, I was shut down and told that I was conflating the article or looking "too deep" into a particular text.

Being told this over and over not only caused a dip in my confidence to speak up for myself, it also discouraged me from participating in the classroom.

Just as I had been deprived of my history and culture in previous academic environments, even here, at an extremely diverse university, I was being shut down. Whether my professor was intentionally silencing me or genuinely thought that nothing was wrong with the lack of representation, it still had a lasting impact on my education and how I viewed the course.

Unfortunately, my experience in that class was not unique to that one course or to the university as a whole. When a particular segment of students is consistently shown that their history and identities aren't important, that narrative becomes internalized. What becomes internalized also becomes taught.

I am trying in my day-to-day life as a Black woman who applies intersectionality in all possible forms to live in a way where I feel seen, heard, respected, and valued. That starts with gaining understanding and empathy from professors who are educating me and who I hope would be willing to also learn from me and others.

I continue to do my part to foster understanding by seeking to be the best version of myself—taking a stance on what matters by writing articles for the school newspaper; assuming student leadership roles; and aiming to travel the world to enhance my worldview and to help advance my activism.

I'm not sure where this journey of exploration and advocacy is leading. I just know that I must keep going because it matters, and so do I.

*"In leadership,
I cannot assume
that good employees know
how to be great employees."*

A Lesson in Leadership
Nothing Is Wasted
By DaNika Neblett Robinson

Teachers lead. Leaders teach. This process is cyclical, and nothing is wasted.

My desire to be a teacher started in pre-kindergarten. Being a lover of words, I enjoyed hearing my teacher read, helping us to phonetically pronounce lengthy words as well as to write them out on the chalkboard.

After lunch one day, I pulled out my red-and-blue soft vinyl mat and blanket to lie down for story time. Most of my classmates were snoozing before the last word on the final page was read. My mind was preoccupied. I was on a mission.

Quietly, I reached above my head. Fumbling while trying not to make too much noise, I grabbed two chalk nubs and immediately stuffed them into my pocket.

When I got home, I quickly dropped my book bag, raced to my bedroom, grabbed my teddy bears, and one by one, I lined them up on the floor.

Class was in session.

Digging into my pocket, I was relieved to find the

chalk nubs intact, ready for me to scribble on the smooth side of my chest of drawers. I repeated the words I heard my teacher speak earlier that day while I practiced the formation of letters and numbers.

Nothing wasted.

By the time I turned nine years old, my family determined that I was a very good reader. Oftentimes, it has been said that practice makes perfect. I suspect being diligent in reading to my teddy bear "students" every day strengthened my ability to read at a fast pace, recognizing that comprehension is also key.

My paternal grandmother, Theresita C. Neblett, became a pastor in the seventies, at a time when women were told they could not lead a church. As a result, my parents were not surprised when at age nine, Grandma Neblett tapped me to teach the children in our church. Sure, I was a mere child myself, but teaching my teddy bears made me a fast reader, a skill my grandma may have thought would benefit my peers.

From then on, my childhood Saturday afternoons were filled with Sunday School preparations. I practiced reading scriptures and lessons from the adult Sunday School books. I was determined that stuttering over words would not be my downfall. Not fully understanding *thee* and *thou* or how to appropriately pronounce *Nebuchadnezzar,* king of Babylon, would not stop this ambitious nine-year-old future teacher.

Nothing wasted.

During those times, I was certain I would go to college and become a schoolteacher. My mom, who was passionate about home economics, gave me two choices: She would buy me a sewing machine or an electric typewriter.

A sewing machine? What would I possibly do with a sewing machine? She likely thought I would be interested in making my own clothes and bedroom curtains, just as she had done in her early years.

Nope. Definitely not interested.

I opted for the electric typewriter, although my typing skills were nothing more than pecking out words one letter at a time. In middle school, I took every business-oriented elective class possible, which increased my typing proficiency and business acumen. Even though my mom could not afford to purchase a computer, that electric typewriter was the tool I used to spearhead my career.

Nothing wasted.

In high school, my interest in the business world pushed my early dreams of being a teacher farther away. I participated in a career shadowing program. But the options my business teacher provided were of no interest to me, so I randomly chose to shadow a medical transcriptionist.

I spent an afternoon observing a medical transcriptionist, a blind woman who worked at the local Veterans Affairs hospital. I was fascinated by her ability to listen to doctors speak in her ear, using a foot pedal to move her recording device back and forth to ensure that she accurately captured every word, while typing without looking at her fingers. But I was mostly intrigued because she was able to effortlessly do all of this without the ability to see. Although the career shadowing experience was interesting, being a medical transcriptionist was not my chosen career. I simply fulfilled a class assignment.

Yet, months later, when I became a teen mother, my initial career goals shifted. I transitioned from dreaming to surviving. A few years after high school graduation, I was able to land a job as a medical transcriptionist, a career I served in for almost a decade.

What I know now is that nothing I did to prepare myself for a career as a teacher, medical transcriptionist, businesswoman, or even a fast typist was wasted—it was simply repackaged.

When I found out that I, an honors student with lofty plans, was pregnant with high school graduation on the horizon, I was devastated. I feared I was going to miss out on life.

What I didn't realize was that the same passion and curiosity that had served me as a preschooler who "borrowed" chalk for my teddy bear students still burned within me. Even in this season of seeming setback, nothing would be wasted.

I went on to become a mother, a wife, a loyal and loving sister-friend, and yes, even a teacher. Today, I am both a teacher and a leader.

Nothing wasted.

The many lessons I've learned by being a mother, wife, and sister-friend have prepared me to become an *effective* teacher and leader. One of the most important lessons I have learned is that no matter what comes, it is important to continue focusing on your personal growth as you journey through life and to share what you have learned along the way.

Mothering an infant is different from serving as the mother of a teenager or young adult. Being a good wife in the honeymoon phases of marriage is different from standing as the wife dealing with a marital crisis. Sister-friends do not meet on day one claiming to be sister-friends; those relationships come with the evolution of time, trust, shared experiences, and connection.

As I learned firsthand, and eventually studied in a doctoral program at one of Virginia's leading universities, women should not take for granted the transferable skills they possess that can aid them in leading in various arenas. We have the ability to empower others to become better versions of themselves by using what we already have in our tool belts. Certainly, being a mother, wife, or sister-friend has taught us many lessons that we can incorporate into our interactions with those we are entrusted to lead.

Leadership experts like John C. Maxwell have made it clear: "People are your most appreciable asset" in any workplace. He also asserts that leaders must be diligent about investing in their own development. "If you want to be successful, you have to truly value people, not just what they can give you. Value them consistently, and you will fulfill an intrinsic need in their life and yours." In addition, "people are only your greatest asset if you're developing and engaging them."

Engaging with people transforms you and the people you are interacting with. Sometimes that can be instantaneous or over a long period of time.

High-performing teams and organizations exist because leaders are willing to teach. Sydney Finkelstein wrote in a *Harvard Business Review* article: "If you're not teaching, you're not really leading." Employees need to learn more than the nuts and bolts of a job. They need to be taught soft skills that strengthen the organization's culture, which positions each person to realize they are interconnected. And, through the interconnected relationships, they can learn from each other while developing innovative approaches to their daily work.

Being a leader requires you to know your family, your colleagues, or your employees, and to understand their needs. Some leaders have opportunities to forge meaningful one-on-one interactions, while others can only connect in group settings, due to the level of their leadership position. In either case, it is important to be intentional as well as allow the teaching to organically happen. Knowing when to transition in and out of those relationships is imperative.

Being a mother has taught me how to empower people to be independent. When they were younger, my two children needed me to guide them on completing homework assignments and to keep them involved in extracurricular activities. As they reached high school and were only years away from college, I recognized the need to be nearby to ensure homework assignments were complete, while motivating them to finish their work without my daily guidance. Abrupt changes when going to college would not be ideal because I could not physically be present to ensure that they dotted their *I*'s and crossed their *T*'s. They needed to be equipped prior to arriving on campus.

Now that they are young adults, my parenting skills have transitioned once again. Telling them what to do at this stage of their lives will not work. Discreetly sharing my pearls of wisdom is what they need. I use this same skill set when leading people at work. My ultimate goal is to give them the tools they need to be successful in their respective roles. Just as I have done over the years with my children, not only do I display the desired behaviors for my direct reports, I also make sure they fully understand, from beginning to end, how to complete a task or effectively interact with their peers.

Being a wife has helped me appreciate that everyone has a past that is completely different from my own. You could marry a person who had a childhood filled with love or perhaps they experienced middle-child syndrome, where they always vied for attention. Their path to adulthood could have led to experiencing college roommates or the need to work to make ends meet. Even more so, they could have made unhealthy life choices or realized that everything their parents told them was true.

Learning to be patient—without judgment—as I watched my spouse's transformation has strengthened my ability to do the same for those I lead. I recognize that I have to allow them time to realize the lessons being taught, and that is not an overnight process.

Sister-friends provide a safe space for transparent conversations, venting, sharing solutions to a problem, and relaxation. They allow you the opportunity to disconnect from work while still talking about work.

Sister-friends give you tools to use when you return; sometimes providing another perspective that you never entertained in your psyche. And, because you return from your retreat refreshed, you are a better advocate for others to do the same, in whatever manner makes the most sense to them. I have enjoyed being on the giving and receiving end in my sister-friend relationships, and again, nothing wasted.

In leadership, I cannot assume that good employees know how to be great employees. Maybe a past supervisor made them feel inadequate, and my role is to build them up. I may see something in them that they have never seen within themselves. My patience is needed as they pursue their metamorphic journey to greatness.

Building relationships with my employees ensures they are open to hearing what I have to say. When teachers are in the classroom and students are speaking, they do not typically cut them off mid-sentence. That behavior only causes a person to shut down and feel as if they do not have a voice.

In the workplace, I recognize that employees are the ones in the trenches doing the work. They may have a better idea of what is needed to create success.

As the leader, it is my job to listen, assess the possibilities, and empower the team to move forward in a new direction.

Leaders teach. Sometimes technical skills. Other times soft skills. Leaders have to determine whether the lessons are intentional or happening organically. The most rewarding aspect of being a teacher-leader is when an employee comes back to share with me how something I said or did changed their perspective.

One of my favorite parables is about ten people who had a skin disease and desperately wanted to be healed because they were not welcomed in public spaces. A leader gave them specific instructions on what they needed to do to be healed. On their journey, the scales began to fall off their bodies because of their obedience. Only one of the ten returned to say thank you.

As a teacher-leader, you may not always hear about the transformation of the individual. Even they are not certain when the change took place, but they listened to the voice of their leader, and as they went about their days, there was a metamorphosis. No matter the circumstances, hold fast to your desire to empower them, knowing that true change will manifest. Even if they do not return to say thank you.

There are times that I reflect on my life and remember that little girl who "borrowed" chalk nubs from her pre-kindergarten class because of a strong desire to teach her teddy bears at home, simply using the smooth side of her chest of drawers. That little girl grew up, and some of her dreams seemed to fade away due to the transitions of life. When she thought all was lost and her dream to be a traditional teacher in an elementary school would not come true, she eventually embraced the fact that her workplace would serve as her classroom.

In her current executive leadership role, the woman who was that little girl is not required to create a lesson plan or teach to state educational guidelines. Life experiences serve as the curriculum from which she teaches. She is only required to seize those opportunities. Today, she—I—can tell others that despite the twists and turns, nothing was wasted. I have an opportunity to teach daily, and I remain grateful for the truths that are evident in what I do with love: Teachers teach. Leaders lead. Leaders teach. Class is always in session.

Journaling Break

*"Whatever the situation,
we must all embrace self-care,
even if it includes
an unpopular choice."*

Finding Peace in Tough Choices
By Njeri Mathis Rutledge

One of the most challenging aspects of womanhood is making tough choices. At some point, life presents all of us with opportunities to make difficult but radical decisions. Maybe it's a divorce, a medical procedure, changing careers, resigning from royalty, or withdrawing from the Olympics.

Many women struggle against being people pleasers and tend to put others before themselves. When we prioritize ourselves, we can be paralyzed by guilt or by the inevitable fallout. Five years ago, I was faced with making a tough choice—navigating a relationship with an estranged and dying parent—and I found myself fretting about the potential consequences.

I had not spoken with my father in almost three decades when he called to tell me he was dying of pancreatic cancer. He wanted me to fly across the country from Texas to Boston to see him. Because of our complicated and distant relationship, I said no.

I had not viewed myself as a daddy's girl since I was seven years old, when my parents separated and divorced. I have dim memories of sitting on my father's shoulders when I was younger and recall visiting and speaking with him only occasionally after our family splintered. I don't remember if the relationship between us faded gradually or ended abruptly. I just know it ended, and it hurt.

I recognize that countless people have amazing relationships with their dads, including many of my friends. When they tell me about their wonderful father-daughter bonds, I wonder all over again what that must feel like. I watch my own daughter interact with her father, my husband, with a mixture of wonder and envy. I am grateful that she has a loving and present dad, of course, but sometimes lament that I missed out on that kind of joy.

Yet, when my father reached out in his final days asking to reconnect, I knew that doing so wouldn't fill the parental gap I'd been living with. I was taught by my mother and in church that selfishness is horrible, and that it is better to put others ahead of oneself. I realized that saying no to a dying man would make me look like an awful person and that I might receive pressure from certain family members to show up, despite how I felt.

Even so, I chose self-care. I could not ignore my belief that going to visit my father would not be best for my mental health.

Saying no can be difficult, especially when the decision is questioned or criticized. However, much of my relationship with my father was centered around disappointment, so I stuck to my guns. What is best for one person may seem crazy to someone else. Nevertheless, sometimes making an unpopular choice, especially when people think you're making a mistake or inconveniencing them, is not an act of selfishness, but an act of courage.

I made my decision after considerable reflection and helpful conversations with my therapist and discussions with my husband and mother. With their support, I was able to lean into what felt best and right for me.

In the months leading up to his death, I spoke with my father several times, and in our final conversation, I knew it would be the last time we would talk. He was weak and fading.

I told him I loved him—and I meant it. I had decided to cherish the fleeting moments we shared when I was a little girl—activities like going to get ice cream, riding a bicycle, and talking on the phone. My choice allowed me to say goodbye to the person I knew as a child without experiencing the pain of hearing others reminisce about the man that I, as an adult, never fully experienced or understood.

This is not to say that my choice was easy. My heart was indeed heavy when my father died. Time had run out, and he was never going to be the father he could have been.

I did not want to be around other family members because I knew we were mourning on different levels. I wanted to be alone. Some life events like grief and pain are not a societal performance, but a deeply painful and complex journey.

And then, I made an even more difficult—and

questioned—choice. I decided not to attend his funeral. I didn't see my refusal as being vindictive. My mourning process was as complex as our relationship had been.

The hardest part was telling my family members. I called a few relatives on my father's side and informed them of my decision. I am sure that my uncles, my father's brothers, were disappointed, but they indicated that they understood. However, my father's only sister was furious.

My mother and maternal aunts were mostly inquisitive. They asked me repeatedly, "Are you sure?"

"Yes, I am positive," I responded each time they queried me.

One of my maternal aunts even offered to fly from Nashville to accompany me to the funeral in New Hampshire. In the end, the most important earthly voice I listened to was my own.

But I had been to funerals before. I knew what to expect. Person after person would stand up and describe a man I had never fully known. They would all know more about my father and his life than I did. That reality hurt too much for me to sit through. So, in saying no to attending his service, I was, in essence, saying yes to myself.

I appreciate this quote by an unknown author: "You will know you made the right decision when you pick the hardest and most painful choice, but your heart is at peace."

I am a woman at peace.

Whatever the situation, we must all embrace self-care, even if it includes an unpopular choice. I still believe I made the right decision for myself.

I encourage you to lean into your difficult moments, listen to your heart, reflect on the wisdom granted you, and choose your best direction with a sense of clarity and peace.

"Being a shoulder-giver
is just as rewarding
as having had shoulders
on which to lean and stand."

Nana's Shoulders

By Stacy Hawkins Adams

T he experience isn't the same for everyone, but when many first-time moms hold their newborn in their arms and peer into that tiny face, something inside shifts. Their world begins to fall into B.C./A.C.—also known as "Before Child" and "After Child."

That was quite true when my first child, my daughter Syd, was born in the late 1990s. My then-husband and I were living in Virginia, a place that had become home because of our careers, far from family in our native Arkansas. However, we had become entrenched in the community and our church enough to have developed special friendships that felt like family. So when we learned that we were expecting a baby, we knew we had a village of support surrounding us. He would continue in his demanding job in the healthcare field, and I would have our baby and return after twelve weeks of maternity leave to my beloved, yet also demanding work as a journalist.

As the calendar chipped away at my days of leave and my infant daughter's smile and personality awakened, so did my bond with her and my desire to not miss a moment of her development. Yet, we were a two-income household; plus, I loved writing—it was as much a part of me as my DNA. I had already arranged, prior to her birth, to work from home several days a week and would only need partial care. Little did I know that it would take three tries before finding just the right fit for both Syd and her dad and me.

We started by hiring a sitter who could care for Syd two to three days a week in her home, which, to me, felt more like a family atmosphere (something I intentionally sought out since we lived so far from relatives). And while the sitter cared for other children, too, the majority of them were older and arrived at her home after school.

That first day of drop-off was a non-event for Syd, but caused the usual first-time mom parting trauma for me. And when, during that first evening and many in the weeks that followed, my baby girl slept incessantly after coming home, I fretted that she wasn't getting enough rest during the day. I followed my instincts and sought out another caretaker.

This time I landed on an older lady at my church who lived alone, was retired, and was delighted to have the company of a sweet baby a few days a week. All was going well, until several months into the arrangement, this woman became ill and could no longer continue to care for Syd.

Frustrated and perplexed, I shared my woes with my friend, Nita, who is my daughter's godmother. I admitted to Nita that I was close to quitting the job I loved—writing for a daily newspaper where I covered social justice issues that were close to my heart, including stories about people working their way off welfare, efforts to provide children with free health insurance, state laws and policies designed to keep kids safe in daycare, and efforts to support women fleeing domestic violence. I valued the career I had carved out for myself and how it allowed my purpose to intertwine with my passion, but I loved this little girl more, and if I needed to leave the newsroom for good in order to raise her in the way that I felt was fitting, I would do what was necessary.

Nita sought to help me brainstorm other options so that I could keep moving forward with my plan to work fulltime, with a few days at home and a few in the office. At some point, Nita mentioned my plight to her mother, a retired seamstress who also attended our church and spent her days volunteering with several ministries, including serving in the church's Monday through Friday soup kitchen.

Ms. Williams had a head of silver curls, a beautiful smile, and a spunky personality anchored in ready quips that flowed with the confidence of a woman who had claimed her right to say and do as she wanted. I saw her at church most weeks and greeted her with a smile and hug and light chitchat, but we hadn't spent much time together otherwise. So when Nita told me her mother would be willing to care for my daughter, I was surprised and grateful.

Ms. Williams offered to give up her daily work at the soup kitchen and watch Syd three days a week, and we agreed upon the fees for her service. Because she was located closer to my former husband's job, he had drop-off and pick-up duties, so I would often call Ms. Williams during the day to check in and get updates on how she and Syd were faring.

Before long, a special bond developed between the two of them, and at some point, Ms. Williams declared what she wanted "her baby" to call her—the same name her grandchildren used, Nana. And a fitting name it was, given that my daughter's maternal and paternal grandparents all lived an eighteen-hour drive away. They, too, doted on Syd, but mostly from afar, so it was a blessing to have this daily nurturing from another senior who was growing to see her role as more than that of a caregiver.

I can't describe the sense of calm and joy this gave me because intentional, extended family means everything when you're a transplant to an area and don't have any around—especially when you're raising a child. The cliché *it takes a village* is a well-worn phrase, but it is true. Not only was I able to finally place my daughter in the arms of a loving grandmother-like figure several days a week, but Nana's wisdom, values, and life lessons also came with it. We became an extended part of her family beyond Syd's godparents who were already our family friends to others who surrounded her, including Nana's sons and daughters-in-law, sisters-in-law, and cousins.

Being able to go to work and focus on my career because I knew someone else's loving focus was on my child helped me flourish in my own purpose. A couple of years after Syd's birth, while she was still in Nana's care, I was invited by my editors to pen a weekly column for the newspaper, which went on to become extremely popular and cemented my role as a journalist who cared about the community in which I lived. And when my son, Jay, was born just after Syd went off to preschool, it was a no-brainer: He would take her place in Nana's arms.

I realized what a gift it was to have her support on his first full day in her care, just after he turned twelve weeks old. My return to the newsroom happened to be on September 11, 2001. Minutes after I settled at my desk, a photographer came running through the expansive newsroom yelling and searching for the remote control to turn on the large TV. A plane had hit one of the twin towers in the heart of New York City. As he and I stood before the screen, taking in the live breaking news coverage about the first incident, we saw the second plane fly into the other tower, and instantly, like the rest of America watching, we knew we had witnessed a terrorist attack.

As a well-trained journalist, I went into reporter mode, realizing I'd need to help tell this story from the perspective of those in my community. I received marching orders from my editors about where to go and who to interview—the leader of a local mosque who was a source of solace to the local Muslim community.

I lost touch with my then-husband and others due to cell phone transmission being cut off and radio waves being silenced, and the only thing I felt settled about was the fact that both of my babies were in the care of people I trusted—Jay with Nana and Syd at a small, faith-based preschool nearby, where I knew her teachers loved her and would keep her safe. That confidence allowed me to serve others through my writing that day and in the days that followed, when I not only wrote news articles, but also inspirational columns about the tragedy, loss, and trauma that had occurred on September 11 to try and bring some semblance of meaning and hope to readers.

About nine months later, I awoke at three o'clock one morning with an urge to resume my childhood dream of writing fiction—an effort I had undertaken in fits and starts after my daughter's birth. This time, I felt a clarity and eagerness to follow through, and six weeks after I got that early-morning nudge, I had completed a very, very rough manuscript from which I could mold and shape something eventually worthy of publication as a book.

When Jay was three years old and Syd was six, my very first novel, *Speak to My Heart*, was nationally published. I went on to write ten more books (as of this publication), including my award-winning novel *Watercolored Pearls*, my *Essence* bestseller *The Someday List*, and my Target Recommended Read novel *Coming Home*. Those early books placed me among the few

African American women writing faith-based fiction at that time, and I flourished in a space that allowed me to write about social justice, women's friendships, and personal growth.

I continue to hear from readers who, as a result of reading my books, say they have been led to reconnect with estranged relatives, improve their lives in some way after the characters' journeys resonated with them, leave abusive relationships, and even reconsider their thoughts of suicide. I also consistently receive opportunities to speak to groups and deliver keynote messages before audiences across the nation and teach at writing workshops far and wide.

This exciting new journey as a journalist-turned-author occurred mostly after my children had left the care of their beloved Nana. But what I know—and what I make sure they know—is that these possibilities were able to unfold before me *because* of Nana. Had she not been willing to alter her daily routine and also open her home and her heart, I may not have continued with a career that has given me opportunities to reach, and in some way impact, thousands.

As a result, I ultimately view any successes that I claim as Nana's successes, too. In her own way, walking in her calling to be a giving and nurturing soul helped fuel my purpose to do so in a different way. There are nanas and aunties and cousins and friends just like Margaret Williams all around us—using their seemingly common gifts, yet contributing so significantly to a greater good that they can take some ownership in producing.

My family's Nana is no longer living, but she lives on in the continued evolution of the purpose she helped me maintain and in the next chapters taking shape for my two young adults who are making their own unique marks on the world with her love and values baked into them. We all stand on Nana's shoulders.

I could go on to share stories of countless other women whose mentorship, listening ear, prayers, guidance, and wisdom have visibly and quietly helped me grow in tremendous ways, simply by being themselves and extending themselves without condition. Along with having shared my gratitude with them verbally and in other tangible ways, I seek to do it every day by remembering how they have helped me rise and see over the horizon, whether long term or for a season.

My best way of paying these gifts forward is to offer my shoulders to other women and girls, both in my circle of influence and through my writing. The more I mentor, advise, listen to, pray with, and love on others unconditionally, the more I realize that being a shoulder-giver is just as rewarding as having had shoulders on which to lean and stand.

It's all relative. It's all relevant.

I'm grateful that the circle continues.

Journaling Break

*"Before there was
Naomi Sims, Iman, or
Naomi Campbell,
there was Terri Springer."*

My Aunt Terri
Fashion's "Black Stallion"
By Wanda S. Lloyd

For women of a certain age who may have followed the fashion industry many years ago, the name Terri Springer is likely familiar. She was the first dark-skinned model ever hired by Ebony Fashion Fair, the fabulous and extravagant traveling show that put the clothes of famous global and up-and-coming African American designers on Black women. The models selected for the show rocked the runway in two hundred cities across the United States, in Canada and Europe every year.

Before there was Naomi Sims, Iman, or Naomi Campbell, there was Terri Springer, a stunningly beautiful, statuesque, chocolate brown woman of great dignity and poise, and a lover of social graces. After her modeling career, Terri became my aunt by marriage.

When she passed away in July 2021, *Ebony* magazine described Terri in this way: "As one of the first fashion models with a darker complexion, her melanated skin paired with her statuesque figure earned her the affectionate title, 'The Black Stallion.'"

In the Fashion Fair shows, Terri was styled in haute couture of such bright colors and dramatic features as to elicit verbal audience gasps and reactions of "wow" when she hit the runway—stepping high, twirling fast, and flashing a big smile with milky-white teeth that punctuated her dark complexion.

Fashion Fair models wore clothes designed by runway-famous fashion houses, the likes of Christian Dior, Yves Saint Laurent, Oscar de la Renta, and Valentino. Sometimes the Black models wore gowns that cost thousands of dollars, even though Fashion Fair founder Eunice Johnson, wife of Johnson Publishing Company founder John H. Johnson, had to use creative tactics to get some of the white designers to sell to her. Yet, as Eunice Johnson opened doors for Black models, the show also highlighted African American designers who initially found it difficult to show their clothes on signature fashion runways or in high-end stores. Some of these Black designers were Stephen Burrows, Lenora LeVon Riley, and Rufus Barkley.

Going to a Fashion Fair show was an experience that wowed audiences and modeled for girls and young women like me that we were black and beautiful, competent and extra special in our community—lessons we didn't always get in the larger society. In Savannah, Georgia, where I grew up, and in other cities where I went to the show as a young adult, we knew that the price of our Fashion Fair tickets would include a one-year subscription to the monthly *Ebony* or weekly *Jet* magazine, the signature products of Johnson Publishing. It was the company's clever way to market the magazines and guarantee their placement on the living room coffee tables of thousands of Black households, and likewise, the magazines served as a branding machine for the traveling fashion show.

Eunice Johnson created not just a show. Fashion Fair was an extravaganza. Beginning in 1958, the annual show became a way for local Black sorority chapters, black colleges and universities, church groups, and social clubs to raise money for service projects. Over the show's fifty-one years, Black women (and sometimes entire families) would prepare for weeks to determine the fancy—sometimes flamboyant—attire they would wear to the show, often the social highlight of the year. For more than five decades, Fashion Fair ticket sales raised $55 million to support local charities' public service programs and scholarships.

Terri loved traveling with the show and all of the glitz and glam that came with touring. When she reached her forties, however, she retired and settled into a new life as the wife of Watson Walker, my mother's brother. Terri moved to Columbus, Ohio, where he was a surgeon in private practice. By then, Uncle Watson was a divorcee and the father of four adult children. Sometimes the elders in my life have said of couples generally, "He's quite a catch for her" or vice versa, meaning one or the other may have married up a notch or two in society. In my opinion, when Terri and Uncle Watson married, they were equally a catch for each other.

He was a handsome doctor, educated at two of the nation's best HBCUs—the Nashville-based historically black Fisk College (now University) and Meharry Medical School. Like me, Uncle Watson grew up in Savannah during the Jim Crow years, when separate societies dictated where and how we were educated, the neighborhood where we lived, where we worshipped, shopped, and appreciated cultural events. After his education, Uncle Watson never returned to the South to live. In Ohio, he was elected multiple times to the school board, and as chairman, he helped lead the system through the period of integration. By the time he and Terri married, he was well respected for overcoming the challenges of segregation in his career and fighting against it in civic arenas. (I write more about Uncle Watson in my memoir released in 2020, *Coming Full Circle: From Jim Crow to Journalism*.)

When I met Terri shortly after they were married, I loved her immediately. She was gracious, loving, and giving. Because she became my aunt in my adulthood, I didn't get to see her often. However, whenever we connected, she willingly answered my questions about her modeling career.

I learned so much more about her early years after her death in 2021, shortly after her ninety-third birthday, and thirty-one years after Uncle Watson's death. Terri's roots were also in the South. She was

71

born in Sylacauga, Alabama, a white marble bedrock quarry town where life was hard, especially for a family with five children. When she was very young, her mother passed away. Terri was sent north to Cleveland, Ohio, to live with an older sister. After high school, Terri completed cosmetology school. While working as a hairstylist, she took classes and graduated from a charm and modeling school.

Sending girls to charm school was once a common practice in families that wanted their daughters to learn the social graces and etiquette for becoming proper young women. In Savannah, I went to charm school twice before I graduated from high school. It was where we learned to stand up and walk straight, often balancing a book on our heads to force a smooth gait. We were taught to sit properly, legs crossed at the ankles, never at the knees. Charm school taught us how to set a proper table for meals, using the utensils correctly, preparing us to host elegant dinners at home and for attending formal occasions.

I can only imagine that Terri's charm school experience was similar to mine, which probably made her a good choice for Fashion Fair and also a more than suitable match for a doctor in a community where she would become a frequent hostess for parties, attending important social events and as a member of social clubs. Terri was a proud member of the Charms, Inc., and The Sophisticates, two national organizations of African American women who sponsor social, cultural, and business activities and programs.

She was also an amazing cook, something to which I can attest as I still prepare a couple of recipes she taught me when my husband and I visited her in Columbus, or when she visited my family.

And even in her later years, she was beautiful. Through her eighties, she was still eye-catching when she dressed to leave home, even if it was for a trip to the grocery store. When Terri said something like "Let me get my cap," she would often come out of the bedroom wearing an elegant beret or a baseball cap embellished with colorful sequins or beads. Sometimes she would put on a plain dress or a simple white blouse, but by the time she added a pair of long shiny earrings and a belt with a statement buckle, it was as if she were about to step on the runway again.

My greatest memory of Terri is how she embraced our family—my mother and me, and later my husband and our daughter—as if we were her own flesh and blood.

I was in my early twenties when my mother called to say Uncle Watson had remarried. I was living in Rhode Island at the time, working as an editor in my first daily newspaper newsroom. I told my mother I couldn't wait to meet Terri, so we arranged to both fly to Columbus to visit the newlyweds.

At the time, they were living in a small condo, likely a one-bedroom place because I remember sharing a pull-out sofa bed with my mother in their living room. Years later, the next time we visited them in Columbus, the Walkers were living in a roomy mid-century ranch-style house with a pool in the backyard. That's when I first recall Terri as a gracious hostess, an accomplished cook, and a great friend.

She and Uncle Watson enjoyed playing cards and other board games, and it was Terri who taught me how to play Scrabble, a word game I still enjoy. She took me to a market in the tony German Village in Columbus, where she showed me many kinds of sausages, years before my husband and I were able to travel to Germany. Her lessons prepared me to understand some of the cuisine on that trip.

Terri talked to me constantly about the importance of traveling and being exposed to different cultures. She wanted me to visit more places, and she was proud when I told her about my travels to France, Germany, Canada, and across the United States. It was because of Terri's stories—and her encouragement—that I made it possible for my daughter, Shelby, to travel abroad several times with student groups.

Terri often told me stories of her travels with Fashion Fair. But I had to learn by reading on my own that when their touring bus would visit cities in the Deep South in the 1950s and 1960s, they would send some of the models who were light-skinned, women who might even pass for white, into convenience stores to shop for snacks and supplies. It was a way to avoid exposing darker women like Terri to the humiliations she and her own family might have encountered in her early years in Alabama.

Terri constantly urged me to join some of the high-society clubs and organizations that she thought would be good for networking in my career as a newspaper journalist. I reminded her that I became a member of Delta Sigma Theta Sorority, Inc. while I was a student at Spelman College. But apparently that wasn't enough for Terri. She wanted more for me.

"I want you to be a member of The Links (an international organization of Black women that focuses on friendship and service)," and she urged me to join one of the groups to which she belonged. For many years I resisted joining more groups, but in 2015, I was invited and I became a member of The Links, Incorporated. Terri was overjoyed.

In the decades after Uncle Watson's passing, Terri continued to visit us and support our family. She traveled to the various cities where we lived—Alexandria, Virginia; Greenville, South Carolina; Nashville, Tennessee; and Montgomery, Alabama. Sometimes I invited her to be my plus-one at social events.

One of those gatherings was the annual corporate-hosted holiday party during my time as a senior editor at *USA Today*. The party was held on the thirtieth floor of the corporate headquarters for Gannett, *USA Today*'s parent company. Terri enjoyed the live music, the elegant fare, and the extravagant decorations.

That's when she first saw me socializing, greeting colleagues, and meeting new people at an event that probably had as many as two thousand coworkers and invited guests. When we returned to the house that evening, Terri told my husband, "Wanda sure knows how to work a room." She had that same broad smile I've seen in so many photographs of her when she was on the runway.

Years later, while I was serving as the founding executive director of the nonprofit Freedom Forum Diversity Institute at Vanderbilt University, a new program that taught journalism to second-career students, I invited Terri to join us in Nashville for the grand opening of our new building and the launch of the program. This event was for a much smaller group than the *USA Today* holiday party, and it was not nearly as difficult to keep up with me. For most of the evening, Terri was perched in a comfortable seat in the lobby, and from time to time I would walk through that area. I saw her sitting there, just watching me with pride and that signature broad smile.

When my mother passed away in 1997, Terri immediately flew to Savannah to join my husband, our daughter Shelby, then thirteen years old, and me for the funeral. Mine is a small family. My mother was the last surviving Walker sibling, and as an only child, I had no other relatives to join us. After the service, when we were in the funeral home car, Terri looked over at Shelby and me and said, "I'll be your mother and your grandmother from now on. I'll be there for you."

And she was—there when Shelby graduated from high school and college; there when I had a surgery that required a longer than planned recovery and she came to cook and care for us; there whenever we needed her or when we had something to celebrate.

When I tell people about my life journey with Terri Springer, the famous model, I listen as they rave about how much they admired her career.

"I remember my mother taking me to the Ebony Fashion Fair as a child," wrote Stanlie James, one of my Spelman College classmates, a retired university administrator and professor, and herself a chocolate brown woman.

Stanlie reacted to my social media post upon Terri's passing in July 2021. "It was the first time I ever saw a dark-skinned model (what a revelation to know that we could be beautiful). The second revelation was that we looked beautiful in bright jewel tone colors. We did not have to limit ourselves to wearing dark colors like black or navy blue or brown just because we had dark skin."

If ever there was a testimony to Terri, that was it for me.

Shortly after Terri passed, I called one of her close friends to tell her Terri was gone. Audrey Smaltz was one of the Ebony Fashion Fair commentary narrators. Terri connected us years before by giving me Audrey's phone number.

After Audrey got past the shocking news with agonizing sadness, she composed herself, and she told me some of her memories of Terri as a Fashion Fair model: "When Terri walked out onto the stage, the audience went wild. Terri stole the show!"

I hope future dark-skinned black girls who want to be models—or scientists or teachers or hairstylists, for that matter—will know that there once was a Terri Springer who broke barriers for them so they would always know they are black and beautiful and smart.

Colorism, a form of prejudice based on skin tone, has plagued Black people for centuries, whether by external discrimination or self-inflicted setbacks. My daughter Shelby and I chose different and unique career paths—me as a newspaper journalist and Shelby as a buyer for some of the nation's largest retail companies. For Black women who have often been judged or marginalized based on skin color, the barriers that Terri Springer broke on one of the biggest stages during the Jim Crow years will likely resonate within us for the rest of our lives.

*"One thing I have learned
on this journey we call life
is that we will all change,
whether we want to or not."*

Keep Getting Better

By Jackie Hunter

Years ago, as a teenager, I heard some of my classmates say, "I'll never change." Those words were uttered with pride, as if remaining as they were was a meaningful—and likely—aspiration. Even though we are now in our sixties, some of us still say it with pride. At our fortieth class reunion, when I once again heard, "I'll never change," I chuckled because I remembered a picture I had seen in a magazine of a tattoo on the wrinkled hip of an elderly woman that said *forever seventeen*. Really? At sixty-plus years old, I could not be happier. I've changed, and I am a better version of my former self. One thing I have learned on this journey we call life is that we will all change, whether we want to or not. So why not embrace, and even create some of the changes that are inevitable?

Physical changes are a given. We won't have much control over them. Some of us might notice at some point that we need to begin using reading glasses. As for me, sometimes, I pass a mirror and do a double-take because I see my mother looking back at me. People in their forties now call me ma'am.

As a child, I remember asking my Aunt Lucille, "How did you get so old?"

"Keep living," she would tell me. "Keep living."

There is more than one way to look at that statement, you know. It could mean *Do nothing, and old age will catch up with you.* Or, it could mean *Embrace life, and live it to the fullest.* I choose the latter.

For me, living life to its fullest means to embrace change. To be clear, I don't just mean to age gracefully. I think it's wise and important to use the time we have on this planet to continually set goals for ourselves. In fact, I believe in setting goals high so that I am always reaching for a better version of myself.

The New Year's resolutions I declare each January have served as the inspiration I need to propel myself—forward and higher. Through the years, I also have developed some simple strategies for reaching my goals and making positive changes in my life. I often ask myself two questions: "What do I need to learn?" and "Who do I need to know?"

A true goal should take us out of our comfort zone. To accomplish it, we need to learn something new, by taking a class or reading a book, which are easy pathways to knowledge. (These days, the internet and YouTube are also worthy sources.)

When I decided to become a science fiction author in 2016, I read quite a few books and articles about how to create realistic characters and develop exciting plots. I even took writing classes at local community centers and online. I got as creative as possible to learn the new skills I needed to succeed.

To meet the people you might need to know, consider joining an association, a club, or even a country club, then find a mentor. It's important to share the energy of a variety of high-performing people because if you're always the smartest person in your group, how will you ever reach your fullest potential?

Once you've answered the questions, "What do I need to learn?" and "Who do I need to know?" it's time to map out a plan. We must get past fears of failure and work the plan. Besides, any failure you experience along the way is often an opportunity for growth.

So how do you work the plan? I have heard that a goal or task without a deadline is but a dream. If you feel overwhelmed by your goal, break it down into smaller tasks, and give yourself deadlines for each.

I have also heard that people without a plan most certainly will fail. Don't let that be you. Remind yourself of your goals by creating vision boards and doing some pillow talk—affirmations to remind yourself that you can do it.

Your vision board can be a poster or it can be digital. Cover it with pictures showing what you want for your life. Pillow talk is a goal written on paper that you place under your pillow. When you go to bed at night, it is the last thing you read; when you awaken in the morning, it is the first thing you read. These written messages and the accompanying evening and morning habits are constant reminders of what you want to accomplish.

Did you know there is science to back up the adage "Fake it till you make it"? The science says if you believe you can accomplish something, your brain will make the neurochemicals needed to make it happen. Henry Ford said, "Whether you think you can or think you can't, you are right. So, believe in yourself and watch good things happen."

Spiritual growth is also important to me. For many people, that is not the case, and I respect that. For me, deepening my spirituality is as critical as personal growth and career growth, and in my search for answers to the many questions I've had along my spiritual journey, I've accepted what has made sense for the time and experiences that fit my particular decade of life.

Reading from an inspirational book or watching a spiritual video daily adds to my peace of mind. Expanding my spiritual growth, leaves me radiating peace and joy.

As a spiritual being, I live as if my body is a temple that should be maintained and treated with love and respect. Toward that end, I have always engaged in some form of exercise and maintained a healthy diet.

My exercise routine may involve aerobics, weightlifting, and stretches. This part of my life has been so much fun because through the decades, my cardio activities have gone from cheering in high school to modern dance in college to belly dancing and kickboxing in midlife. Now in my "seasoned years," it's Zumba, yoga, and daily walks. This regimen has kept me strong and flexible, so I am able to live as an independent senior citizen. Just two years ago, I decided to uproot from my native Virginia for life on the West Coast and a move to a city that fits my life choices as a vibrant retiree and author.

In terms of diet, I've always been a proponent of eating plenty of fruits and vegetables, and now I realize I do not need to eat meat at every meal. In fact, these days I only have meat, usually poultry, for lunch. Since I began this diet I've noticed that my eyes are brighter, probably because my liver doesn't have to work so hard. These dietary changes have kept me free of any drug regimen.

I believe developing hobbies should be an important part of one's self-actualization. Some folks relish their jobs and do not set aside time for hobbies, yet making time for hobbies will help career-driven people become more efficient in their professional lives. Hobbies give the mind a stress relief. My hobbies of oil painting and writing are revitalizing. After spending time painting or writing, I can take on the stresses and challenges of life with renewed energy.

A challenge to all is to learn something new daily, whether about your chosen career, your spiritual path, or your hobby. Eat healthy and get plenty of exercise. By following these simple suggestions, you will be living and growing into the life of your dreams. Wouldn't that be fabulous? And always remember, change is inevitable, so you might as well create the changes you want in your life and keep living.

Afterword

And there you have it – a book of personal reflections penned by women who are intentional about connecting with themselves and others, and about growing and thriving in each stage of life – amid their successes, setbacks, and all.

After reading, we hope you've had some *aha* moments, chuckled a bit, experienced some hope, and felt like you've been communing with friends. For the journey through womanhood requires all of that; and as you've consumed our stories, it is our wish that they've made you more appreciative of your own.

May you flourish in all that you are and get excited about all that you are becoming.

Acknowledgements

The writers and cover artist of this book sincerely thank the following supporters:

Daphne Maxwell Reid, the multi-talented photographer, author and venerated actress best known as *The Fresh Prince of Bel-Air's* "Aunt Viv," for her kind support in penning our Foreword;

Chandra Sparks Splond for her editing services, and the

Focused Writers Membership Community, which includes several scribes who are not featured in this book, due to joining the group after the "master class" journey to producing this anthology was underway. Their support and enthusiasm for this project are appreciated.

Contributors

Stacy Hawkins Adams is an award-winning author who routinely mentors other writers. Her women's fiction novels and inspirational nonfiction books, essays and articles

infuse readers with confidence in their own stories. Her eleven titles thus far include nine novels, a nonfiction devotional book, and a compilation of her original quotes and musings. *Watercolored Pearls* has been a featured title in college coursework; *Coming Home* was a Target stores "Recommended Read" and *The Someday List* was an *Essence* magazine bestseller. Stacy curates a blog called LifeUntapped.com, and in addition to leading the Focused Writers Membership Community, she teaches at writing conferences in Richmond, Virginia where she is based, and around the globe. Learn more at StacyHawkinsAdams.com.

 **Dawn Edge Campbell** is an accomplished artist whose dynamic paintings and illustrations have been exhibited throughout the Mid-Atlantic region. She is the cover artist for several books, including *On Womanhood: Connecting and Thriving In Every Season* and *Abound: Principles for Next Level Living*. While occasionally exploring other genres, her passion is bringing music, performance, and artistic design to life in her work. A graduate of Virginia Commonwealth University's acclaimed art program, this Richmond-based artist often leads workshops and teaches classes and enjoys helping others explore their artistic side. Learn more about Dawn's work at dawncampbellartllc.com.

**Nailah-Benā Chambers** is a student at the University of Maryland, Baltimore County. She is majoring in Global Studies with a Chinese language minor and is a member of the Humanities Scholars Program. She is active with her university's Student Government Association and writes op-ed articles for the school newspaper. Nailah-Benā is also a member of several campus organizations, including the Black Student Union and the Black Lives Matters movement. She is a native of Richmond, Virginia.

 **Margo Clifford** is a crusader for children's rights and empowering young minds to think, create, and believe in themselves. As an educator for more than 40 years, she witnessed the amazing resilience that children have to overcome obstacles and seeks to infuse those truths in her writing for and about young adults. Margo, who lives in Richmond, Virginia, is currently writing a novel about two young brothers who are navigating the perils of homelessness. Connect with Margo online at mecliffordblog.wordpress.com.

Jackie Hunter became a novelist after retiring from a 31-year career as a public school administrator and middle school teacher. She writes young adult fiction that makes science engaging, just as she sought to do as an educator. Her novel, *Lost in the Red Hills of Mars*, has been compared to esteemed author Ray Bradbury's work. She hosts a YouTube show called *The Rippy Effect*, for which she interviews young scientists and doctors to inspire girls and youths of color to consider careers in STEM (science, technology, engineering and mathematics). Having served as a science teacher, assistant principal and summer school principal during her career, Jackie's passion for getting students excited about science endures. She is CEO of The Rippy Effect, LLC, a not-for-profit company that secures support to send middle school students to Space Camp and STEM camps. Jackie is based in Las Vegas, Nevada. Learn more at TheRippyEffect.com.

Wanda S. Lloyd is an award-winning journalist and author whose career spans four decades and includes stints as an editor at seven daily newspapers, including *The Washington Post* and *USA Today*. She retired as executive editor of the *Montgomery Advertiser* in Alabama and returned to her hometown, Savannah, Georgia, where she became an author in 2020. Her memoir, *Coming Full Circle: From Jim Crow to Journalism*, has received much acclaim, and she has co-edited with novelist Tina McElroy Ansa a collective of essays entitled *Meeting at the Table: African-American Women Write on Race Culture and Community*. She and Tina also co-host a podcast on Spotify and YouTube called *2 Old Chicks Who Know a Lot of Sh*t!"* Wanda's numerous awards include induction into the National Association of Black Journalists Hall of Fame and an Honorary Doctor of Humane Letters from her alma mater Spelman College. Learn more about Wanda at wandalloyd.com.

Rita Flores Moore is an award-winning inspirational speaker, life coach, and author who has years of speaking and presenting experience. Her highly rated presentations blend humor and motivation,  and empower audiences to achieve more. As a life coach for seniors, Rita motivates individuals to embrace the phases and stages of change (and possibility) that come with aging. A resident of Mebane, North Carolina, she is the author of an essay titled *No Greater Love,* published in an anthology titled *Love-Hope-Faith*. Rita is the producer of *Purpose Driven Video: Launch Your Brand and Increase Visibility*, which is an Amazon bestseller. Learn more at RitaMooreSpeaks.com.

Jacqueline Johnson Owensby is an author, Bible teacher, Christian life coach and educator. She is the founder and president of Women In Need of Empowerment  (W.I.N.E.), a ministry that equips women to live 'in' purpose. She is also the co-founder of The Ministry of Reign (M.O.R.), a 501(c)(3) faith-based organization that provides coaching and education through foundational teachings that "Build people to activate purpose." Learn more about Jacqueline, who is based in Hampton, Virginia, at stayonthevine.com.

DaNika Neblett Robinson is the author of *The Metamorphic Journey*, a novella that explores three teenage mothers' quest to succeed. This fictional work is based on her experiences of becoming a teen mom, first-generation college student and ultimately the recipient of multiple academic degrees, including master's and doctoral degrees. The Metamorphic Journey is also the name of a movement that DaNika founded to foster individuals' personal growth. Additionally, she is the founder of Wailing Women Ministries, a nonprofit organization that provides book scholarships to female high school seniors. DaNika is a higher education administrator and expert in transformational leadership who speaks widely about the benefits of diversity, equity, inclusion, belonging, leadership, and justice in the workplace. Learn more about DaNika, who lives in the Richmond, Virginia area, at themetamorphicjourney.org.

Njeri Mathis Rutledge is a Harvard-trained legal expert, writer, speaker and researcher who has honed her knowledge of timely issues related to law, race and criminal justice. She routinely shares her perspective and insights on the cultural touchpoints of this era in the opinion pieces she writes for *USA Today*. Njeri is a former prosecutor and a tenured professor at South Texas College of Law in Houston, where she resides. She loves mentoring emerging writers through a national organization called The OpEd Project and through the Star Program, which is operated by her undergrad alma mater, Spelman College. Learn more about her work at njerirutledge.com.

Belinda Todd is a longtime writer and world traveler, who served as an international flight attendant for 31 years before retiring and switching careers—becoming a high school English teacher and adjunct college professor of literature and writing. She has since  retired from those second and third careers, and now spends her time writing occasional lifestyle pieces for publication, penning and delivering sermons, teaching yoga, serving as a freelance actor, volunteering in her community, and spending time with family and friends. She resides in Petersburg, Virginia and can be found online at linkedin.com/in/belindatodd.

Cassie Edwards Whitlow is a military wife, mom of two, educator, songwriter, singer and author. Her two novellas are titled *One Wish* and *Temptation*. Currently based in Las Vegas,  Nevada, she has lived in several states and also in England, a stint that fueled her creativity. She is the founder of a community group that offers emotional support to military families, and in her first year of teaching in Las Vegas, she was selected as her district's 2020-21 New Educator of the Year for middle school. Learn more about Cassie at cassiewhitlow.com.